At
Some
Point

WISCONSIN POETRY SERIES

Sean Bishop and Jesse Lee Kercheval, *series editors*
Ronald Wallace, *founding series editor*

At
Some
Point

David O'Connell

THE UNIVERSITY OF WISCONSIN PRESS

Publication of this book has been made possible, in part,
through support from the Brittingham Trust.

The University of Wisconsin Press
728 State Street, Suite 443
Madison, Wisconsin 53706
uwpress.wisc.edu

Printed in the United States of America

Library of Congress Cataloging-in-Publication Data

Names: O'Connell, David, 1974- author.
Title: At some point / David O'Connell.
Other titles: Wisconsin poetry series.
Description: Madison, Wisconsin : University of Wisconsin Press, 2025. |
Series: Wisconsin poetry series
Identifiers: LCCN 2025016625 | ISBN 9780299355449 (paperback)
Subjects: LCGFT: Poetry.
Classification: LCC PS3615.C643 A93 2025 | DDC 811/.6—dc23/eng/20250606
LC record available at https://lccn.loc.gov/2025016625

For
Julie and Elizabeth,
always

Contents

I.

Late at Night, I Watch *The Blue Planet*   3

We're Thinking of the Black Hole at the Center of the Galaxy   4

Fresh Air   5

I'm Happy Because My Daughter Is Sad   6

Intervale Cemetery   7

Period Piece   9

Frank O'Hara   11

The Physician   12

I'm Calling 911!   13

Hunt   15

You Must Act as Though You'll Live   17

In Spring   18

Let's Talk About the Weather   20

II.

Watching My Wife Parasail   27

The Yard Is Full of Light   28

I Was Startled It Was Death   29

We Rush to See Their Movies   30

After   31

The Forecast Calls for Snow   32

My Friend Comes Back 33

This Is How It Happens 34

In College, We Were Assigned "The Dead" 35

In Case You Were Wondering 37

Watching My Daughter's Tap Recital 38

The Past Isn't What It Was When It Was 39

The Rational Animal 41

You Were My First Fox 42

Cathedral Ledge 43

III.

Minor Planets of the Inner Solar System 47

Oh My Goodness, Here Goes Your Body 49

Procedure 50

Avalanche 52

As If There Were Lessons 53

How to Tell the One About Fatherhood 54

This Time 56

Emitter 57

I Read the Dead Are Returning 58

The World as It Is 59

Encore 61

All Summer, the Rain 63

Love Song 64

Starter Home 66

When I Hear It's a Buyer's Market 67

The Elegant Universe 68

Acknowledgments 69

I

Late at Night, I Watch *The Blue Planet*

Here come the seeming billion fishes
schooling somewhere equatorial,

all snack-sized and shiny as the foil
on a Hershey's Kiss. I'm astonished

they bundle up this way, as if hawking
themselves to the hungry passersby,

but as the big fish lunges into frame,
it's the sudden dazzle of their teeming

fleeing every which way that leaves
the lummox gobsmacked long enough

for them to go where he won't follow.
Oh! Where have I seen this before

if not with me? Again, today, so many
choices flashed by the whole universe

seemed possible. And I wanted it all.

We're Thinking of the Black Hole at the Center of the Galaxy

leaning back in our lawn chairs, the August constellations
crowded by a crush of stars, the Milky Way in soft focus
like a Glamour Shot. A couple and a couple at the end of the day
watching our kids zip sparklers back and forth across the lawn
like satellites or meteors. It'd been a story in the paper,
evidence of a supermassive black hole, and so we throw it back
like tequila shots and wade past our depth—me, deflecting
to Kubrick's Star Gate sequence, those long light smears
on Bowman's helmet, Julie, pulling both cords of her sweatshirt
taut, saying our bodies would be stretched to angel hair
if we were yanked into that hole. Then Janet's telling us
how she imagines this supermassive black hole is like the hole
at the end of a vacuum cleaner. *And right now*—Saturday evening,
our kids growing restless, minutes from boredom, then, maybe,
those nudging arguments of who found who, who was safe,
and for us, at least, the hour's drive home, I-95 congested
by the night shift roadwork just beginning, Julie and I
talking quietly in front, reviewing the evening, overwhelmed
by the obvious, how we've all changed, how we won't ever
be as young as we were, our daughter, grass-stained,
her hair wild with static, slouching down in the back seat
pretending to sleep as she listens in just as I did at seven,
those long drives to Maine, picking up things half understood
in the language of grown-ups—*this black hole*, says Janet,
*is hoovering up stars and planets like so many pretzel crumbs
ground into the shag.* We're full. Everything off the grill
is hitting the spot. And Mark, back to Kubrick's Star Child,
is leaning in to share his fanboy theories of what it all means,
though I'm not listening, not really, because it seems right,
that vacuum, because I, too, have plucked stray fuzz clinging
half in, half out of the attachment's rim—and yes, this is
how it feels, year-by-year, to be drawn to the irresistible thing.

Fresh Air

You know this interview
  is just part of the job,
as taking on the part
  was also part. You're no fly
on the wall to his therapy.
  It's just another movie
he's shilling. Still,
  he's one of our species
exuding that X
  that coaxes far-flung attention
to his considerable orbit
  for as long as he shines. So
you tune in with millions
  to lose yourself
in the hour of anecdotes
  he serves like those exotic
entrées you've seen in print
  but always mispronounce.
How American
  to love what lays you low:
by sign-off, your good life
  small as a desert isle
laid bare by his rising star,
  a little FM static
lapping your shore
  where you listen, doing
dishes, not really hoping,
  but hoping you might be found.

I'm Happy Because My Daughter Is Sad

at the end of the movie, the same way,
before she was born, I was sad

when these credits rolled and the lights
in the theater came up slowly, gently

tugging me back from that other world
where now on our couch my daughter

is wrestling with tragedy. *It gets me
every time*, I tell her, heartened

that my twelve-year-old is miserable
they'll leave it this way—the actors

and director—that this will always be
the only ending. Behind us, night

and cold press up against the glass
as I think how, in the park downtown,

there is the statue of a young woman
in uniform—not a person, but enough

like a person to imagine what, for her,
this moment in the dark must be like.

Intervale Cemetery

One of those New England pocket sites,
it takes some effort to imagine, more
than a century ago, it held the heart of grief

over and over, the minister intoning
the rite above a body in its coffin
attended by mourners, then lowered

into this ground now overrun with weeds
and last year's leaves. The only cheer
comes from the small flags that dot

the grass, calling out the Union soldiers.
Otherwise, no keepsake or flower
commemorates the dead. A few are buried

before one of the marble, waist-high
family markers still drawing attention
to those surnames that must have once

meant something in this town. Most
have simple stones, gray as bad teeth,
jutting every which way or fallen flat

along the gently rising slope as if trying
to join the departed. A regional word,
coined in the 1840s, *intervale*

suggests this spot afforded the grieving
a view of the river, long since blocked
by the neighborhood. Its backyard fences

hem the graveyard's lowest edge, while,
incongruously, the local middle school
rises on the higher side, its teachers' lot

bordering the ridgeline. This year,
pandemic measures require masks and bar
the use of lockers. Unable to carry

their overloaded backpacks, my daughter
and her friends wheel them to school
like battered airline luggage, struggling

to pull them along their shortcut
through the cemetery. As they cross,
she tells me, they'll each, out loud, say

I'm sorry, though she's not sure who
started this, and, pressed, rolls her eyes,
embarrassed to admit the reasons they do.

Period Piece

We're living days we know
will end up in the movies.

Some evening, years on,
we'll be in the dark, many of us

recalling or trying to recall
where we were in these moments

we'll be reliving through a lens
and through those actors

whose faces we'll line up
beside the faces so familiar to us now.

These are the memories
we'll haul into the theater

that'll keep us from becoming
entirely lost to the suspense of the film,

while the film's good script
keeps us from losing ourselves

to our recollections, softened by time,
of these days now vibrating

with the tension of a single violin
scraping up an accelerating scale

over interstitial shots
of the instantly recognizable,

all of which insist
upon the gravity of these days

we're living hour-by-hour
with an anticipation I can't imagine

any director will quite capture
since then

we'll know how this must end.

Frank O'Hara

reading you, I am not jealous
of your renown half so much

as that cast of actors, painters,
friends breezing in and out of

the poems. It's late. It seems
you had the life. I'm working

these days from home and on
my lunch half hour, I stroll

from the clutter of the study
to the kitchen. O I envy you

your city, too. That possible
metropolis. Despite the years,

know the glamour of your
labor stays au courant—lines

so couture, who but you
could pull them off? Tonight,

mid-June, the oscillating fan
tsking *no, no, no,* your words

hit me the way my bent elbow,
struck, will suddenly sing

pain, then go to tingling
so that all of me is focused

on some feeling coming back.

The Physician

when asked, splutters,
then gasps, hacks,
his index finger
held up, *a moment,*
it says, for he can't

catch his breath, is
bent over, shoulders,
head, neck jerking
with the effort, fist
at his mouth as if

yanking a fishing line,
its hook sunk deep
in a branch of his
wet lungs, his eyes
shut tight against

the pain of it, panicked,
the desperate straw
of his throat sucking
at dregs, at what
there is, there is, yes,

breath, another, all
over, it's over, and
knowing this, he sighs,
asks what was it again
that's on my mind.

I'm Calling 911!

In the '80s sitcom version
of our lives, it'd be
her child-star catchphrase,

pouted out and arms crossed
in close-up as the pots and pans
crash down on her mom

or the misplaced rake pops up
to send me staggering
back while the laugh track

lends its heavy hand to push
the comedy. And in real life,
it *is* almost funny how,

since she's known the protocol,
it's been her knee-jerk move
—a little blood, a venial

bump, or hearing someone
curse in pain—to start yelling
again, for all the world

to hear, she's going to call
an ambulance. My daughter.
Once, in traffic, I saw her eyes

roll white as she went limp
against the padded shoulder
of her safety seat. Her mother

whipped into a parking lot
where I brought the shot
down hard on my child's thigh.

In the soapy drama version
of our lives, those fraught seconds
I count the epinephrine in

before lifting the injector,
I'm entirely the hero
as, eyelid flutter, our daughter

returns to us. The truth?
I knew she'd eaten what
could kill her but, the rash

mild, felt it best we drive
ourselves to the hospital—insisted
my wife not make the call.

Hunt

My heart, all night, knocks
    against my ribs,
claiming suffocation,

claustrophobia, and how
    it hates the dark.
A week, I've barely slept,

and when I do, I dream
    it's out—wet lump,
amphibious, blinking up

from a puddle on the floor, dull
    as a stewed tomato.
For hours now, I've shush-

shushed my jittered heart
    as if it were
a pet afraid of thunder,

a magician's snare roll
    I'm trying to slow
to adagio. But it

wants none of this, rabbits
    at the faucet's drip,
keeps claiming there's a dog,

nose down, who set it
    running in the womb,
a hound it can't outpace

if it must carry me,
    and carry me,
the way it has till now.

You Must Act as Though You'll Live

You must act as though you'll live,
though you will not live

and can imagine when you're gone
the few stories that will be told

about your life, each a bright thread
that, in time, will fade

until all that's said about your life
is genealogy, your name

or only your initials
beside those of the ones you love

and call by name
and struggle to understand.

It is for them that you must trust
when there is so little to win your trust

that it matters. Not just this rain
you feel falling

but knowing it's fallen before
far from here under this same sun.

In Spring

when the sun slips,
it takes the light
as if it were a fabric

pulled slowly over
the edge of a table.
Day's warmth follows

as the birds go silent,
and the wind combs
its fingers through

new leaves. Hours
pass this way,
the houses going dark,

the river of traffic
running dry until
a shut car door

is enough to catch
the ears of those parents
in dim bedrooms

who cannot sleep
because what's possible
sounds like this,

the engine turning
over, its unknown
driver roaring

somewhere
that feels like summer
and will not wait.

Let's Talk About the Weather

In a word: wilting. Not yet June
and a string of these days already,
high 80s, humid, like a necklace
of ears, trophies of the dawning
apocalypse. Too dramatic? Let's talk

about the sky—no clouds, the way,
flying, you get above the weather,
so, though grounded, I'm trying
to picture how far they're up
Everest again. It's climbing season

in Nepal, the weather a balmy
4° by my phone. From world over,
they throw in big money to gamble
everything, knowing if they die
they'll be unrecoverable, and all

for that exquisite peak. They *need*
good weather. Snow (phone again)
is falling there now. I wish them luck,
especially those souls torturing
themselves, as I'd be, with racing

thoughts of baking places—Al-Ahsa,
Saudi Arabia (104°), Linguère, Senegal
(104° also), though it's only 74°
in Hamilton, Bermuda, where I once
honeymooned. It was so much hotter

then, disembarking, the pastel hotels
rising like amphitheater seating
above a near-neon North Atlantic
where the equatorial sunlight leapt.
That weather, held close nineteen years

in memory, was almost impossibly
thick, heavy, and I was dressed for it,
but not the ship's fine dining (shorts
prohibited). For three days, docked,
I was consumed with finding slacks

on the island. Try it. A treasure hunt,
or was. Sweat (then, now) is the body
talking back to weather, as is shiver
and teeth chatter—all this, syntax
of the language that, with strangers,

we lunge for. Case in point, this morning,
a salesman stopped by to talk fences,
and, at once, it was the weather—
swapped forecasts, shared hopes
for weekend sun—that greased the wheels

of commerce. I just may buy his wares
to fill the new-made gap where pines
once stood, the arborists' crane swinging
blighted twenty-foot trunks up and over
our neighbor's roof. She'd had it done,

she told us, so when she's gone,
her son won't have the fuss. Come
hurricane season, no trees looming,
I'll sleep easier. Now, beside her
garage, I can see the Virgin Mary,

arms raised in benediction, sky-blue
robes mid-flow, presiding over tulips
and azaleas. I hadn't realized Ms. S
was religious—Catholic? Safe guess,
so much of RI is, as are my parents

in Erie, PA (67°, cloudy). Mostly,
their weather seems to travel east,
the texts my mother sends so often
full of heat or cold that arrives here
days later. Sometimes, I picture rain

following the I-90 traffic past Niagara
through the Leatherstocking Region
to the Mass Turnpike, then over
Providence to my own backyard.
I know it's the tilt of the planet

that causes such weather, the perfectly
imperfect warming giving rise
to high/low pressures, winds
rushing oceans, leaving doldrums
that doomed ships. All the way back

—Cambrian explosion, Sturtian
glaciation—before we ever were,
the weather, surely, was already
shaping a fundament we feel in
our genetic code, so it makes sense

that we make sense of our emotions
by calling them stormy. This evening,
the meditation app near-whispered
all my loneliness, joy, desire, grief
might be observed as passing clouds,

an innate meteorology. OK. I guess
that checks: most days, the part of me
that's water pulls toward rivers while
something (what?) other hungers for
stillness amidst my interior weather.

II

Watching My Wife Parasail

From shore it seems the ocean's eager everywhere
for sun. I can almost hear the wavelets bark
as they crowd and nip the boat's stern where she waits.
Even with binoculars, I can't determine if it's joy
or apprehension Julie's feeling as the engine chumbles
like a smoker's cough, then whines up to speed
and the sail, directed by the towline's arrow, rises
like some impossible bioluminescent jellyfish
drawing stares and gestures all along the beachfront.
Look! As if caught in its tentacles, she dangles, bare legs
kicking as she's hauled above the boat masts, above
the decommissioned lighthouse set like a Saturn rocket
on the farthest spit of sand. Higher than the wheeling gulls,
she finds the apex, and I realize, suddenly, this too
is something I want, and that I want so much already,
as they slowly winch her in, and the world goes still,
and I wave; I wave and clap this stranger back to earth.

The Yard Is Full of Light

to bursting, falling down throats
of lilies that simmer in orange

and royal yellow. The season
is at its most aristocratic, careless

with this light it can't spend
fast enough, wave on wave of it

washing over your paperback
left in the grass, warming itself

like a stone. That still. All afternoon,
I've told you what I remember

of childhood summers. Not much,
we discovered. Light-drunk,

the bees did their lazy acrobatics,
dandelion fluff held currents

we couldn't feel. There was the time
and then another. All of it ended

up here: our yard, the July sun,
this unexpected moon, caught

by daylight, pressed to the sky
like a fingerprint against cold glass.

I Was Startled It Was Death

I was startled it was death
I'd been singing all morning
under my breath, scrambling
the eggs, steeping Earl Grey
for breakfast with my wife, death
I'd been carrying like a jingle
or Top 40 chorus, its melody
infinitely catchy, insistent,
vaguely parasitic, its lyrics
surfing rhythm, slotted into
rhyme, over and over, a half
hour or more, all Saturday
ahead of us, the morning sun
shining when Julie protested
with a quick laugh, though
wincing too—*no, please,*
I just got that out of my head.

We Rush to See Their Movies

when they die read their novels pore over
their oeuvre deep cuts the music saying
also they have passed there was something

that was here now maybe all these years
waiting for this the instant of their absence
not yet callused over so we still feel

the weight of it what they made it burns
our palms like rope we crouch at the lip
the split the mouth belaying them they

two three days gone still descending we
stare down cool air rising though we can't
see them call out reassuring we won't let

go hopeful the echo hollow we know
what must and the line goes slack
is what we hold

After

Because I thought it would
make me less lonely, he said,
that it would provide . . .

and he paused, until his silence
became the silence of those lakes
underground, entirely still

and in a darkness so complete
it would blind you to the hand
reaching out for you. He was

turned from me then, toward
that border of his fields
where a copse of pine trees

was swaying, slightly, nearly
in unison, while the evening
fell, and then we went inside.

The Forecast Calls for Snow

Thirteen is apparently old enough
to indulge in that favorite pastime:
contempt for how things are, how

they're not like the good old days.
My daughter and I are bundled up,
the sky a fading quilt slung low

above the quiet houses. *These kids,*
she's saying, *will never know the joy
of a snow day.* It's true. Tomorrow,

if schools close, the district goes
remote: video classes and online
homework as the plows rush by

and headlights, midday, peer through
a nor'easter's fury. Thirteen winters,
I'm finding, is enough to become wise

and a little wistful as, turning back
for home, the two of us feel closer
the way those growing older

have always felt, finding themselves
on the same side of a divide
watching others drift further away.

My Friend Comes Back

once the house is asleep
because I say it

and seat him in a kitchen chair
under the fluorescents

where he gives me the grin
that meant mischief

in 1992.
That I can't give him a drink

is just one of the limits
we're up against,

as is the fact
he won't tell me anything

I don't already know.
But that's okay

for as long as it takes for the two of us
to rehash good times

now thirty years past,
until I forget

when the conversation
turns,

as it always does,
that those are my words

in his mouth.

This Is How It Happens

Running, you stumble on a lyric
before you catch the melody
of a song telling you twenty-seven

is just as you remember: so much
indecision, heartbreak. Getting old
is what Lisa was saying last week

about living in the city. Those first nights
the sirens woke her in a panic, but now
she sleeps through the night.

In College, We Were Assigned "The Dead"

"That's the rule of the order," said Aunt Kate firmly.
"Yes, but why?" asked Mr. Browne.

—JAMES JOYCE, *"The Dead"*

When I read that Cistercians
slept in their coffins—*you*
do not know the day, the hour
—I was nineteen and remember

thinking it thrillingly nervy,
much more so than robes
or keeping the breviary
or even that impossible vow

of silence. All through my twenties,
I would drop those monks
into dinner party small talk
the way others might mention

Diane Arbus or Fugazi or
how a bird of paradise will
flash its tail in a beautiful
form of ritual. It seemed

at the time more dare than
devotion to lie in the box
that, too soon, would trap you
underground while the insects

slipped in. Something, as teens,
we'd have goaded each other
into risking, like trestle diving
or binge drinking, to prove

death, though surely waiting,
wasn't here today. It was only later
in that uncomfortable decade,
once religion proved a cake

alive with worms and God
became an echo, one night,
alert in the dark, listening
to my heart beat too close

to the surface, I found myself
imagining the abbey's interior
the way someone else might
count sheep. Stone floors,

stone walls, closed doors
behind which each monk slept
so soundly in his coffin
you would be tempted to

bring a pocket mirror close
to check for signs of breath.
It didn't matter that, by then,
I knew Joyce had been pushing

a myth. It was just the idea
I was holding onto, drifting
into sleep, that anything,
with time, might lose its bite.

In Case You Were Wondering

The road's still there, outside and above the city,
offering its elbow from which to watch the lights,
evenings, pop on, and many hours later, wink out,
one by one, until it's mostly just the streetlights

and the traffic lights cycling their three commands
like sergeants after all their men are gone. Summers,
you might still pull onto the berm, sit on the hood
as the engine cools and the metal, cooling, ticks

like the moonfaced classroom clock, though irregularly,
as if time were yawning wide, and you, for applause,
had stuck your head inside its mouth. How romantic
and embarrassing it might be to be there and wonder

again if you were truly satisfied—looking down
on the city, which is really a town—or just in love
with seeming so. You didn't know the difference then,
unlike now, surely, if you went back tonight.

Watching My Daughter's Tap Recital

I think of Mrs. B, my typing teacher
that summer before high school,
and how my mother would drop me off
those too-bright Saturday mornings
to slump before a Smith Corona
in the cool, tiled basement classroom
of the all-boys prep, and I remember
the satisfying snap of the letters
hammering the ribbon to the clean
white page, tattooing their gibberish
(*asdfg*) amid the dropped-coins clatter
of my classmates, all of us stumbling
to keep up with her endlessly patient
encouragement to work the pinky,
semicolon P, semicolon P, over
and over in a gently lilting cadence
coaxing those synapses that free me,
thirty-odd years on, to type without
hunting or pecking or ever much
considering (her routine over, we're
wildly applauding) those drawn-out
hours, that once hypnotic voice.

The Past Isn't What It Was When It Was

the present. It's the past. (Obvious.) But
when we recall it, the past, there it is

all over again. And so we fool ourselves—

make fools of ourselves—foolishly grin
as we lift memories up like caught fish,

confident in our prowess. *Yes, this is*

what happened. But it isn't. Not really.
Take Italy. Newly married, I'm on vacation:

four days, five nights. Then twenty years

race by before my young daughter asks
about the framed photo. And I say, *Oh,*

that's St. Mark's Square. And over there

(I point at the wall, beyond the picture)
is the palace and basilica. I can see that

I'm losing her, so I go and tap the glass

above the campanile, explain in my best
tour guide: *One morning in 190-something,*

it collapsed! She's unimpressed. *Of course,*

they fixed it, and there are bells up there
so loud your mother and I held our ears

like this. I grimace, pantomiming for her

as if I hear them. (I do.) She doesn't
care about this past, but I'm talking now

about the place I ate the soup and the place

I ate the gnocchi—*like pillows*—and explain
about the snow—*It snowed!*—when

my wife, from the other room, says *No,*

you're thinking of Florence. And my daughter,
somewhere in the middle of her parents'

rising voices—good-natured, then digging

trenches—slips away from us, most likely
vowing never to ask about another photo,

even as I go in close to this one, squinting

back across half my life for the evidence
I'm sure, if I look hard enough, is there.

The Rational Animal

There may have been a logic, but it looked flustered,
then frantic, as if embarrassed to be caught flying

past midnight in my kitchen. I don't know
how it felt but tell you I felt some seismic

pulse generations deep within me raise its tsunami
of adrenaline and fury, my badminton racket

flailing at (maybe) rabies zagging till the open window
swallowed it whole,

        and I shut it out, and turned my back,
only, all night, to hear it flit about me in the dark.

You Were My First Fox

outside of storybooks, surprising me
as I turned left off Bear Hill Road
and slowed to be sure you were
what I thought you were. You were,
in fact, a fox. Less red than the fire engine red
of those many illustrations of upright foxes
playing the small-time hood, always
foiled, shaking down the rabbits and mice
and other small creatures I've seen
in the "wild." I say quote/unquote wild
because it's what we do to forgive
our imprecision—the bunny in my 20-by-30
backyard, the mouse in my oil-stained garage.
And then you, in broad daylight, walking
stiffly along the berm of Abbot Run,
most likely sick (and dangerous), though
it felt to me like dignity, or a sadness
so complete you refused to look back
and see what was approaching.

Cathedral Ledge

All afternoon my daughter, wife, and I eddied
in and out of overcrowded shops in a slow stream
of tourists drawn by a shared, unspoken desire
for something more than fresh-tapped maple syrup
or moose T-shirts, moose keychains, felt pennants
sporting antlers, postcards of the mountain range
from every angle, in all seasons. The mountains

rose over our shoulders, a chord of bass notes
bowed slowly under our high-strung pizzicato.
October, the leaves had been the draw, though
they weren't peak yet, we were told. And told. Told
Cathedral Ledge was where to watch the sun
come down, we drove the fifteen minutes up
to find an ordinary backyard chain-link fence

stretched along the edge of a wide shelf of granite
worthy of its name, inviting us to approach
and safely peer over. Below, wind-bit scrub pine
clutched wherever lips of the cliff face pouted
into weather. There would be snow come nightfall.
The incoming clouds were in formation, dropping
shadows across the Saco River Valley. *Look there,*

my daughter, just seven then, exclaimed, pointing
where (it took a moment to register) two men—boys,
really—were tied together and to the cliff with what,
from that distance, seemed little more than thread.
Painfully deliberate, splayed against the rock wall,
by fingertip and toehold they made their way up while
a crowd swelled, lining the fence like a ship's rail,

all of us excitedly whispering as if we might startle
these creatures in the wild. Why climb a mountain?
Because it's there offers nothing that could explain
what we witnessed as, at last, they made the summit,
stripped off shoes and socks, stood barefoot at the edge,
and we returned to our car, reliving what we'd seen,
careful on the winding road back down to our hotel.

III

III

Minor Planets of the Inner Solar System

Overheated classroom, fluorescents
buzzing drowsily, she's telling them
there's always violence in the galaxy.
In the beginning, violence, and science

has tracked the evidence. In their text,
there's Uranus, off-kilter, and Mercury
scarred. Turn the page, and remnants
of the proto-solar system still hurtle

through vast and lonely places. We're
plotting their trajectories, she says,
says if we had the speed and direction
of every potential, then it's possible

we might save ourselves. Next fall,
most here will be flung across the country
by their ambition, scattered and pulled
into ever tighter orbits—universities,

then careers, then families, the future
largely mapped by where they started
and those who came before. It's a miracle,
of course, that we've survived this long,

considering the shooting gallery
through which we whistle in the dark,
to say nothing of those anxious nights
Homo habilis kept watch by the fire.

When did one of us first imagine
we could nudge away oblivion? Minor planets
of the inner solar system, that's what
we've dubbed them. Twenty-three students

in neat rows lean forward, taking notes
about life's gamble, the likely chance
there's one death out there, even now,
predestined for them. There'll be a test

next Tuesday, she warns. The old gum
stuck like barnacles beneath these desks
once burst with flavor. The long arm
of the clock strains to lift the minute.

Oh My Goodness, Here Goes Your Body

Taking on water in the frigid North Atlantic
Far from land or hope of rescue. It will feel
Like a lifetime before it sinks. Years, even,

There will be good reason for you to hope
That the weather will stay mild and the pumps
Will keep ahead of the ocean rushing in

From leaks too numerous to patch. Of course,
You are not a ship. You are a person—
The only creature in the universe we know of

That, when asked, can imagine being this ship
As the wind, at last, kicks up, fouling the rigging
And rending the sails until, quicker than you thought possible,

You will be pulled under,
And the sea will go on as before.

Procedure

There's an odd connection one feels
on a Friday morning in a waiting room
with two other men, both around my age
or just a little older, all three of us
marking time until our colonoscopies—

this man more fit than me, sporting
loafers without socks, and this other man
who arrived late, unshaven, now tap, tap,
tapping his hand on his knee as we all watch
a couple redecorate their home on TV.

And because I've slept so little, and eaten
nothing, and swallowed the twenty-four large pills,
each of which was like a depth charge
you might see in an old war movie,
the barrel rolled off the vessel's stern

while, deep beneath the waves, the crew
of the submarine braces for them
to explode—and they do, and the ocean
starts spraying in—wait! What
was I saying? Yes, there is a comradery

I feel with these strangers who I know
viscerally understand my experience
of the past twelve hours—the intimate
and . . . indelicate confrontation
one will have with their inmost self

sitting alone in the middle of the night
—and this is a bond, though unspoken,
that confers some pluck as, one by one,
like in a troupe's modernist staging
of judgment day, our names are called.

Avalanche

Ally tells me her husband is adjusting,
that they all are, that the diagnosis
is for the right kind of cancer, *if that
makes sense*, and they're trying

to stay positive. This being his third
round of chemo, they have no illusions.
Two days on, they trust he'll feel
the poison. It's like with lightning,

she says, the one-a-thousand, two-a-
thousand before the thunder cracks.
After the first treatment, she couldn't believe
how good he seemed. Back from the clinic,

he'd cut the lawn, fixed the porch step,
told her he felt alive in a way he hadn't
since the tests. Or even before then,
she admits, those long weeks she'd spent

tiptoeing past his symptoms, avoiding
all but the most routine conversations,
lest the whisper of her suspicions
set this avalanche in motion.

As If There Were Lessons

Those were the hours, infected,
we were aware of her body, the fever

wringing out the cloth of her, the sheets
a witness. This was a skirmish

in a war of attrition—win the day,
ignore the lost cause. Is this the lesson?

When I was five, I'd sit on the curb
with a paper-clip hook on a string

to fish the storm drain. What is empathy
if not a found treasure? After illness,

sun. That's what I mean: the lesson
a tchotchke. And her body,

a bird from the nest, as if falling
is what's meant by all this time.

How to Tell the One About Fatherhood

A man and his daughter walk into a drugstore.
That he won't know best is the twist. The setup
relies on a tacky Grim Reaper, its skull white

as disposable utensils, a plastic black cowl
hiding the wire it hangs from above them.
Explain it's October and how the decoration,

triggered by their entrance, shimmies and moans
so that the daughter, just four, buries her face
in her palms. Jump then to bedtime: the girl

in tears, afraid of the dark, the man at a loss.
Understand that the story you're telling
is less joke than trial, that its outcome

will mean one thing to the man and another
to this girl who'll remember her whole life
what comes next. It's death, of course,

that upset her, though she doesn't know one day
she'll die. As will her father. And the father,
through all his *it can't hurt you, I'd never let . . .*

doesn't think he's lying. This is the time now
to pause, leaving space for your listener
to feel for a man who struggles for answers

as he gets in the car and drives his daughter
back to the store in her pajamas. Nearing
the end, take time to sketch the empty aisles,

the long fluorescents humming as if angry
with the night. Take care. Bring them
to this moment cautiously. Not so much

allegory as anecdote. Less anecdote than
ephemera: a father lifting up his child,
saying, *trust me, there's nothing to fear.*

This Time

when she asks where she'll go when she dies,
all her eight years surround her, leaning in,

eyes bright, hands on their knees, as if called
by the crack in her voice. And in the silence

after, as they shoulder in, eager for a sparkler
or magic trick, I know what I say next

will be a worm being pulled from the dirt
that breaks, half squirming deeper underground

and half carried back with these girls
who she was, until one made inconsolable

returns, hands cupped, to whisper her awake
just across the hall from where I sleep.

Emitter

Night seeps in early
and herds the lamplight
into tight corrals.

Somewhere in the world
something died
millions of years ago

and was transformed by time
and weight and heat
until we dug it up

or drilled it out
darker than the dark
crouching at the lip

of each bright circumference.
It's only the money
that keeps the lights on,

the money and the burnt offering
that is the dead thing
transformed again

so that it haunts us,
what it might do to us
and to our children.

I Read the Dead Are Returning

from deep within the permafrost
as if summoned by a planet in crisis.

We're amazed how close they are
to who they were, their shoes still lined

with grass for insulation, their bodies
holding on to the arrowheads

that left them unburied, until buried
without ceremony by the weather.

Warmed by the sun, they begin,
almost at once, to let go. And like ghosts

of our stories, they each have a horror
to tell—a solitary murder,

a village massacre—though time has
dulled their terror. Nearly December,

we steel ourselves for the coming
season, bleed our radiators, crank up

our thermostats. Across my lawn,
a pale morning sun is carving long

shadows as I watch my breath
leave its record in the air.

The World as It Is

Some believe the new math
proves reality is actually

a hologram. And who am I
to argue when I don't know

the language? I speak pig math.
At times, finger count. Failed

this week to help my daughter
with her fractions. *Don't worry,*

you'll never use it in real life,
remember? But now it seems

this math has always been
presiding over smoke-filled

back rooms of the universe,
invisible mover and shaker

knowing what we want
are answers, and that we want

them now. Outside, the street
is darker for the light rain,

and I've cracked the window
to catch the scent of earth

kicked up by water falling
back to us. Nothing is lost,

explained the talking head
last night, asking that we picture

clapped erasers raising
clouds of dust. The math

he detailed says it's possible
for every molecule of chalk

I smacked out in angry
plumes beside St. Mary's

one afternoon in 1982
to reverse and gather again

upon the board—faint, then
clearly remaking each mistake

I'd scrawled that day in class.
Implausible, but not. An act

the nuns would've taught us
wasn't math but miracle

on par with the angels
that appeared—like what,

if not holograms?—to trumpet
what they knew was right.

Encore

Seasoned teacher, the conductor
lifts her baton as one might
a rod to cast a hook: quick

flick. And, with that, music
floods the middle school gym, rising
from center court to the rafters

where banners hoarsely crow
their victories. It's a melody,
says the program, that's held on

three centuries to reach us here
on the uncomfortable bleachers
where we angle our phones

to catch the flautist's big solo,
her instrument threatening
to knock the glasses off

her neighbor as he visibly
counts down each measure
with the concentration

of someone defusing a bomb.
Unkempt and wonderful, the
harmonies are all uneven tween

aspiration and indifference,
a semester's rehearsals, hours
at home spent practicing or

(mostly) procrastinating, until
this, the encore, all evening,
they've been working for.

Low brass notes rebound
off tiled walls. An errant
trumpet just hints at what's

on the page. Most of us—
parents, grandparents,
disgruntled siblings—lean

forward toward the snare drum's
rising storm as, calm captain,
the maestro steers her ship

up the final crescendo: a wave
towering above us that (glorious
cymbals) crashes to our applause.

All Summer, the Rain

   fell every three or four days,
sometimes a deluge, the storm drains
   backing up, the traffic
sending dark waves curling surf-like
   over sidewalks, the gutters
pulling them back like a tide.
   And, once, driving, we saw
someone walking: gray blur
   bent forward, given over
completely to the storm. *This can't last,*
   I murmured, rushing by.
And it didn't, the inevitable August
   sun, sheepish, peeked out
then doubled down its effort so, soon,
   wraithlike, the steam rose up
off hot pavement around you—*oh, holy,*
   I thought, who grew up listening
to sermons about those taken up
   body and soul. Not that I believed,
ever, in those lucky few
   who witnessed this, heads back,
hands shielding their eyes, amazed
   by this life, yes, just then, like us.

Love Song

Oh, that's right—because I'm going to die.
Sometimes I forget. More often than not.
And then, that's right! I'm going to,
sometime. Because . . . I'm going to. Forgetting,
but only sometimes, that's how this works
more than not. And then we wake to snow,

~

quite unexpected, the whole neighborhood quite,
you know. And you say to me, *yes, that's right,*
cream, two sugars. Sometimes I forget. Or
these days, more often, because, you know,
that's how this works. And now I remember
we're going to. Both of us. And there's the car

~

snowed under, looking so unlike itself. It takes
an easy faith to see it. What it truly is. I believe
this morning the whole neighborhood is a fact
refuting last night's forecast. I'm predicting
this icicle by evening will stretch down past
the window, which reminds me—yes, that's right,

~

last night, two or three a.m., I woke to the whole house
moaning in the wind. And I felt warmer beside you
surrounded by this sound, our house, and maybe
the whole neighborhood, the neighborhood houses
and the neighborhood trees all moaning. It was snowing,
but I didn't know. Sometimes, I forget this

~

is how it is with us. Just as I, at times, forget
I, we, are going to, you know. They're saying now
more is on the way by evening. It almost hurts
to look out there's so much sun. I'm going out
to prove the car's still here. You remind me,
yes, of course, coffee. How could I ever forget?

Starter Home

Before us, others called our house *our house.*
We know their names, met their grown children.
At the closing, they said *Mom's house, Dad's house,*

but we were not confused. In one day, our house
was empty, full. If possible, it was more our house

because we thought, *these walls should be blue,*
not green, and we were right. Later, we returned
with the baby, and then years became *these rooms*

where she once and *the times that we all.* Now,
there is our house, and our house, and our house,

so that often when we speak, three doors open
on three rooms where what happened happens
almost as it happened in our house, which we agree

will always be our house, even when it's theirs.

When I Hear It's a Buyer's Market

I don't want to die, but think that I might like to die
here, under this roof, if only so I'd never again
    have to tour another open house
    and peer into a stranger's bathroom, imagining myself
    looking back at me, seated on the toilet late for work.
Because when I add up all of the hours of my life
spent not just in painting bedroom walls
    but in waffling over the colors for those walls
    and waiting for the bored clerk behind the counter
    to operate the paint-spattered mixing machine
    that spins each can like some convoluted metaphor for rebirth,
then I'm not sure I have it in me to begin again
    with the roofer who left our gutters on the lawn
    or the carpenter who built the basement staircase crooked.
It's enough, I think,
    after living in nine houses in three states before the age of twelve,
    and having tacked on four more states, six apartments, and two houses
        since,
to understand, at last, that there's something to be said for my grandfather,
    born on the upper story of the split-family on Ninth Street
    where eighty-seven years later he lay dying
while my father, after moving further and further away,
    raced back home to say goodbye.

The Elegant Universe

I love sitting up with this thick book
for the decidedly non-physicist
because it assures me there is sense
to be found in those absurdly colossal
lassos of gravity, great lariats of orbits
inside orbits, just as there is nonsense
in matter's subatomic peekaboo
that slips every noose. Sentence-by-
sentence, both, at once, are true,
just as it's true that our short history
as told in the small type of these pages
has been one long dawning realization
that every last star in the universe
will go dark. So it's alright with me,
book shut, that nearly everything
I've read has already slid off the table
of memory, and I'm not offended
that, all along, I could sense how patiently
the author was working to coax me
from my ignorance. And if it's true
I don't understand much more of life
than when I started, it's also true
each chapter has been like one of those
warm nights I could hear my parents,
younger than I am now, talking softly
in the next room, and I knew they were
making plans, and that in the morning,
we would all set out to follow them.

Acknowledgments

Grateful acknowledgment is made to the editors of the following publications in which these poems first appeared, sometimes in different forms.

32 Poems: "We Rush to See Their Movies"

Bryant Literary Review: "I'm Calling 911!" and "Watching My Daughter's Tap Recital"

Coal Hill Review: "As If There Were Lessons" and "Avalanche"

Cumberland River Review: "Minor Planets of the Inner Solar System" and "This Time"

I-70 Review: "Frank O'Hara"

Kestrel: "Fresh Air" and "You Were My First Fox"

Little Patuxent Review: "In Case You Were Wondering" and "When I Hear It's a Buyer's Market"

Mason Street: "The Rational Animal"

New Ohio Review: "I Was Startled It Was Death," "Love Song," "We're Thinking of the Black Hole at the Center of the Galaxy," "The World as It Is," and "You Must Act as Though You'll Live"

One: "Cathedral Ledge"

ONE ART: "How to Tell the One About Fatherhood" and "Starter Home"

Ploughshares: "The Elegant Universe"

Southern Poetry Review: "Hunt"

Solstice: "The Physician"

Sugar House Review: "The Past Isn't What It Was When It Was"

Tar River Poetry Review: "Late at Night, I Watch *The Blue Planet*"

Valparaiso Poetry Review: "Period Piece"

Verdad: "Watching My Wife Parasail"

Water~Stone Review: "I'm Happy Because My Daughter Is Sad"

"Hunt" was reprinted in *The Strategic Poet: Honing the Craft* (ed. Diane Lockward, Terrapin Books, 2021).

"I Read the Dead Are Returning" reflects on the article "As Earth Warms, Old Mayhem and Secrets Emerge from the Ice," by Franz Lidz, published in the *New York Times* on November 2, 2021.

"When I Hear It's a Buyer's Market" is dedicated to and in loving memory of my grandfather, Patrick O'Connell.

My deep appreciation to series editors Sean Bishop and Jesse Lee Kercheval, as well as Dennis Lloyd, Tristian Lee, Alison Shay, Jessica Hasan, Jennifer Conn, and everyone at the University of Wisconsin Press who helped shepherd this book to publication.

I am especially grateful to Ronald Wallace for selecting this manuscript for the Felix Pollak Prize. It is an incredible honor to have *At Some Point* be included in the catalog of Pollak Prize titles, many of which I've admired for nearly as long as I've been writing.

Thanks to Jeff Drury for reading the first draft of this manuscript, to Michael O'Connell for reading the final draft, and particularly to Robert Cording for giving me the insights and encouragement that helped me bridge these versions.

Love and thanks to my parents, Patrick and Suzanne, for their support, as well as to my siblings Mary, Stephen, and Michael.

Thanks to Elizabeth, who appears in many of these poems and inspired much of the rest. Most of all, my love to Julie Danho, whose brilliance made this book better.

DAVID O'CONNELL is the author of *Our Best Defense* (Červená Barva Press) and the chapbook *A Better Way to Fall* (The Poet's Press). His work has appeared in *New Ohio Review, Ploughshares, Cincinnati Review, Southern Poetry Review,* and *North American Review,* among other journals. David lives in Rhode Island with his wife, the poet Julie Danho, and their daughter. More of his work can be found at davidoconnellpoet.com.

WISCONSIN POETRY SERIES

Sean Bishop and Jesse Lee Kercheval, *series editors*
Ronald Wallace, *founding series editor*

How the End First Showed (B) • D. M. Aderibigbe

New Jersey (B) • Betsy Andrews

Salt (B) • Renée Ashley

(At) Wrist (B) • Tacey M. Atsitty

Horizon Note (B) • Robin Behn

What Sex Is Death? (T) • Dario Bellezza, selected and translated by
    Peter Covino

About Crows (FP) • Craig Blais

Mrs. Dumpty (FP) • Chana Bloch

Rich Wife (4L) • Emily Bludworth de Barrios

Shopping, or The End of Time (FP) • Emily Bludworth de Barrios

The Declarable Future (4L) • Jennifer Boyden

The Mouths of Grazing Things (B) • Jennifer Boyden

Help Is on the Way (4L) • John Brehm

No Day at the Beach • John Brehm

Sea of Faith (B) • John Brehm

Reunion (FP) • Fleda Brown

Brief Landing on the Earth's Surface (B) • Juanita Brunk

Ejo: Poems, Rwanda, 1991–1994 (FP) • Derick Burleson

Grace Engine • Joshua Burton

The Roof of the Whale Poems (T) • Juan Calzadilla, translated by
    Katherine M. Hedeen and Olivia Lott

Jagged with Love (B) • Susanna Childress

Salvage • Hedgie Choi

(B) = Winner of the Brittingham Prize in Poetry
(FP) = Winner of the Felix Pollak Prize in Poetry
(4L) = Winner of the Four Lakes Prize in Poetry
(T) = Winner of the Wisconsin Prize for Poetry in Translation

Almost Nothing to Be Scared Of (4L) • David Clewell

The Low End of Higher Things • David Clewell

Now We're Getting Somewhere (FP) • David Clewell

Taken Somehow by Surprise (4L) • David Clewell

Thunderhead • Emily Rose Cole

Borrowed Dress (FP) • Cathy Colman

Host • Lisa Fay Coutley

Dear Terror, Dear Splendor • Melissa Crowe

Places/Everyone (B) • Jim Daniels

Show and Tell • Jim Daniels

Darkroom (B) • Jazzy Danziger

And Her Soul Out of Nothing (B) • Olena Kalytiak Davis

Afterlife (FP) • Michael Dhyne

My Favorite Tyrants (B) • Joanne Diaz

Midwhistle • Dante Di Stefano

Talking to Strangers (B) • Patricia Dobler

Alien Miss • Carlina Duan

The Golden Coin (4L) • Alan Feldman

Immortality (4L) • Alan Feldman

A Sail to Great Island (FP) • Alan Feldman

Psalms • Julia Fiedorczuk, translated by Bill Johnston

The Word We Used for It (B) • Max Garland

A Field Guide to the Heavens (B) • Frank X. Gaspar

The Royal Baker's Daughter (FP) • Barbara Goldberg

Fractures (FP) • Carlos Andrés Gómez

Gloss • Rebecca Hazelton

Funny (FP) • Jennifer Michael Hecht

Queen in Blue • Ambalila Hemsell

How to Kill a Goat & Other Monsters • Saúl Hernández

The Legend of Light (FP) • Bob Hicok

World of Dew (B) • Lindsay Stuart Hill

Sweet Ruin (B) • Tony Hoagland

Partially Excited States (FP) • Charles Hood

Ripe (FP) • Roy Jacobstein

Last Seen (FP) • Jacqueline Jones LaMon

Perigee (B) • Diane Kerr

American Parables (B) • Daniel Khalastchi

The Story of Your Obstinate Survival • Daniel Khalastchi

Saving the Young Men of Vienna (B) • David Kirby

Conditions of the Wounded • Anna Leigh Knowles

Ganbatte (FP) • Sarah Kortemeier

Falling Brick Kills Local Man (FP) • Mark Kraushaar

The End of Everything and Everything That Comes after That (4L) • Nick Lantz

The Lightning That Strikes the Neighbors' House (FP) • Nick Lantz

You, Beast (B) • Nick Lantz

The Explosive Expert's Wife • Shara Lessley

The Unbeliever (B) • Lisa Lewis

Radium Girl • Celeste Lipkes

Water Guest • Caroline M. Mar

Slow Joy (B) • Stephanie Marlis

Cowboy Park (FP) • Eduardo Martínez-Leyva

Acts of Contortion (B) • Anna George Meek

Blood Aria • Christopher Nelson

Come Clean (FP) • Joshua Nguyen

At Some Point (FP) • David O'Connell

Bardo (B) • Suzanne Paola

Meditations on Rising and Falling (B) • Philip Pardi

Old and New Testaments (B) • Lynn Powell

Season of the Second Thought (FP) • Lynn Powell

A Path between Houses (B) • Greg Rappleye

The Book of Hulga (FP) • Rita Mae Reese

Surveille (B) • Caitlin Roach

Why Can't It Be Tenderness (FP) • Michelle Brittan Rosado

As If a Song Could Save You (4L) • Betsy Sholl

Don't Explain (FP) • Betsy Sholl

House of Sparrows: New and Selected Poems (4L) • Betsy Sholl

Late Psalm • Betsy Sholl

Otherwise Unseeable (4L) • Betsy Sholl

Blood Work (FP) • Matthew Siegel

Blood Harmony (4L) • Bruce Snider

Fruit (4L) • Bruce Snider

The Year We Studied Women (FP) • Bruce Snider

Bird Skin Coat (B) • Angela Sorby

The Sleeve Waves (FP) • Angela Sorby

If the House (B) • Molly Spencer

Wait (B) • Alison Stine

Hive (B) • Christina Stoddard

The Red Virgin: A Poem of Simone Weil (B) • Stephanie Strickland

The Room Where I Was Born (B) • Brian Teare

Fragments in Us: Recent and Earlier Poems (FP) • Dennis Trudell

Girl's Guide to Leaving • Laura Villareal

The Apollonia Poems (4L) • Judith Vollmer

Level Green (B) • Judith Vollmer

Reactor • Judith Vollmer

The Sound Boat: New and Selected Poems (4L) • Judith Vollmer

Voodoo Inverso (FP) • Mark Wagenaar

Hot Popsicles • Charles Harper Webb

Liver (FP) • Charles Harper Webb

The Blue Hour (B) • Jennifer Whitaker

American Sex Tape (B) • Jameka Williams

Centaur (B) • Greg Wrenn

Interstitial Archaeology • Felicia Zamora

Pocket Sundial (B) • Lisa Zeidner